SEPTEMBER
2023

Homes Around the World

THIS EDITION
Editorial Management by Oriel Square
Produced for DK by WonderLab Group LLC
Jennifer Emmett, Erica Green, Kate Hale, *Founders*

Editors Grace Hill Smith, Libby Romero, Maya Myers, Michaela Weglinski;
Photography Editors Kelley Miller, Annette Kiesow, Nicole di Mella; **Managing Editor** Rachel Houghton;
Designers Project Design Company; **Researcher** Michelle Harris; **Copy Editor** Lori Merritt;
Indexer Connie Binder; **Proofreader** Larry Shea; **Reading Specialist** Dr. Jennifer Albro;
Curriculum Specialist Elaine Larson

Published in the United States by DK Publishing
1745 Broadway, 20th Floor, New York, NY 10019

Copyright © 2023 Dorling Kindersley Limited
DK, a Division of Penguin Random House LLC
23 24 25 26 10 9 8 7 6 5 4 3 2 1
001-333890-Sept/2023

A catalog record for this book
is available from the Library of Congress.
HC ISBN: 978-0-7440-7173-3
PB ISBN: 978-0-7440-7174-0

DK books are available at special discounts when purchased in bulk for sales promotions, premiums,
fundraising, or educational use. For details, contact: DK Publishing Special Markets,
1745 Broadway, 20th Floor, New York, NY 10019
SpecialSales@dk.com

Printed and bound in China

The publisher would like to thank the following for their kind permission to reproduce their images:
a=above; c=center; b=below; l=left; r=right; t=top; b/g=background
Alamy Stock Photo: Gary Blake 35cra, Nathaniel Noir 36-37; **Dreamstime.com:** 1tommas 26-27, Acceleratorhams 10-11,
Rango Alien 34-35, Nathan Allen 1b, Byheaven87 13crb, Christineg 3cb, Rafa Cichawa 15crb, Elena Elisseeva 4-5, EPhotocorp 6,
Golasza 40-41, Tomas Griger 9tl, 11tr, 13tr, 15tr, 16tl, 18tr, 20tr, 23tr, 24tr, 26tr, 28tc, 31tr, 33tr, 35tr, 37tr, 38tr, 40tr, 43tl,
Fritz Hiersche 25tr, Hlphoto 25tc, Icolorfulstone 7cr, Javarman 14-15, Jminka 11crb, Holger Karius 42-43, Lukasz Kasperek 30-31,
Ivan Kmit 28-29, Roman Makedonsky 7tl, Jeanne Provost 38-39, Mariusz Prusaczyk 8bl, Anne Richard 29cr, Saletomic 32-33,
Sfocato 12br, Shargaljut 12cl, 12crb, Stevanzz 16-17, Michael Turner 18-19; **Getty Images / iStock:** E+ / byakkaya 22-23, helovi 13,
Thiago Santos 8-9, tjs11 24-25; **Shutterstock.com:** Laurens Hoddenbagh 27cr, IrinaK 44-45, linlypu 21

Cover images: *Front:* **Dreamstime.com:** Ivan Kmit

All other images © Dorling Kindersley
For more information see: www.dkimages.com

For the curious
www.dk.com

Homes Around the World

Max Moore and Roxanne Troup

Contents

Welcome Home!

What is a home? For some people, a home is a building made of wood, brick, or concrete. It might be on a quiet street with several other houses built in a row. It could be a group of rooms in an apartment building in the city. Or, it could be a home surrounded by green fields without another house in sight.

There are many kinds of homes in the world. What they look like depends on the climate, culture, and available materials in the area. Wherever people live, "home" is a shelter. It protects them from the weather. And it gives them a safe place to eat, sleep, and socialize with others.

Different Purposes

Some homes are made to stand in one place for a long time. They are permanent homes, designed for people to live in for many years.

Permanent homes come in many different shapes and sizes. Some of the smallest—and simplest—are houses made of stone or brick. These homes have one or more rooms inside where one family lives.

Sometimes, a row of nearly identical homes lines a city street. Some of these homes have stood for hundreds of years.

Shipyards

La Boca is a neighborhood in Buenos Aires, Argentina. In the 1800s, immigrants who worked in the shipyards lived here. They built homes out of scrap metal and painted them bright colors.

Buenos Aires,
Argentina

The largest permanent homes are skyscrapers. Many families can live in one of these tall buildings.

Intempo, an M-shaped skyscraper in Benidorm, Spain, overlooks the Mediterranean Sea. The building is 650 feet (198 m) tall and has 47 floors. It has 256 apartments where people can live. Due to lack of funding, it took nearly 15 years to finish the skyscraper.

Benidorm, Spain

Tallest Building
Intempo is the tallest residential building in the European Union.

Other homes are movable. They are made for people to live in for short amounts of time. They are often made with lightweight materials that can be taken apart and put back together as needed. This makes them easy to transfer from one location to another.

Rolling Along

Some movable houses are built on wheels. Owners move these homes whenever and wherever they like.

A yurt is a movable home. This round, tent-like house is strong but flexible. It is made with a wood lattice frame and covered in layers of wool or felt. A waterproof canvas rests on top.

Mongolia

The nomadic people of Mongolia and other parts of Central Asia have built yurts for thousands of years. Traditionally, they herded animals. They built yurts so they could follow their grazing sheep, goats, and yaks.

Different Styles

Often, people build homes in ways that honor the past. Before the 20th century, the Toraja people of Indonesia lived in traditional wooden homes with boat-shaped roofs. Some still do.

These homes are called tongkonans, which means "to sit together." Here, family members gather for ceremonies and to discuss important issues. Tongkonans are not just homes. They have carvings of plants and animals that have special meaning to the family. The homes are part of a family's identity and traditions.

Tongkonans always face north to honor the Torajan source of life. Traditionally, their roofs were made out of bamboo. Today, many of these homes have metal roofs.

South Sulawesi,
Indonesia

Alberobello, Italy

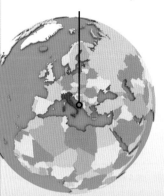

Sometimes, homes help people remember the past. In the mid-14th century, people in Alberobello, Italy, built homes called trulli.

Trulli were made out of limestone rocks collected from nearby fields. The homes had cone-shaped roofs that shed water. No cement held the rocks together. Yet the homes were sturdy and warm. Some people still use this technique to build homes there today.

Many of the original trulli are still standing. They are used as museums and hotels. They show what life was like in the area long ago.

Homes can also reflect the things that inspire people. Octavio Ocampo is a Mexican artist. His brother, Eduardo, was an architect. They were inspired by seashells lining the beach.

Together, the brothers designed and built a special house on Isla Mujeres, a Mexican island in the Caribbean Sea. The home looks like a giant conch shell.

Tall Tale

Taxi drivers and tour guides joke with tourists about how Shell House came to be. They say a giant shell washed up on shore. It had enough meat inside to feed everyone on the island for a week. Later, the Ocampos used the shell to make Shell House.

The brothers named their house Casa Caracol, or Shell House. They used seashells to decorate the inside of the home, too. Everything from curtain hooks to water faucets is made out of seashells. Later on, they built a smaller shell-shaped structure next door.

In the 1920s, a large home was built in Tianjin, China. The home wasn't constructed in the traditional Chinese style. Instead, it featured a mixture of European styles.

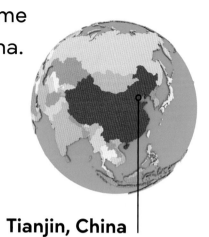

Tianjin, China

In 2002, an art collector bought the house. This man wanted to share his culture with the world. So, he decorated the house with millions of pieces of Chinese porcelain pottery.

The decorations include 4,000 ancient vases, 400 white marble sculptures, and 13,000 ancient plates and bowls. There are also 300 white marble lions. The pieces come from different periods throughout China's history. Today, the Porcelain House is a museum for historic Chinese art and artifacts.

Different Materials

Often, a home's style depends on the materials available to build it. Some ancient peoples built shelters in caves or carved them from rock. Homes like this blend into the surroundings. They are warm in winter and cool in summer. And they make the perfect refuge from danger or bad weather.

Cappadocia, Turkey

Long ago, ash from erupting volcanoes turned to stone. The stone eroded, creating these strange formations in Cappadocia, Turkey.

People dug into the soft rock and carved out underground communities. They had homes, churches, storehouses, and stables for their horses. They lived there to escape from their enemies.

Fairy Chimneys
Today, visitors call these formations fairy chimneys.

In some parts of the world, people still build houses underground. Coober Pedy is a town in the hot Australian Outback. There, summer temperatures can reach 113°F (45°C) in the shade!

Coober Pedy, Australia

To escape the heat, many people dig their homes into the sandstone hillsides. Underground, the temperature stays a cool 75°F (24°C). Opal miners started this tradition some 100 years ago.

opal

Digging In
Sandstone is a
soft rock that is
easy to shape and
carve with hand
tools. Sandstone
dugouts are homes
"dug out" of the earth.

In Iceland, some people build turf houses to withstand the cold and wind. These homes have a stone foundation and a wooden frame. They are covered with grassy dirt bricks called turf.

Iceland

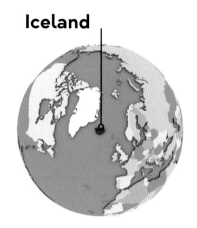

People have built turf houses in this area since the ninth century. Turf is an easy material to find.

Turf houses often have only a few doors and windows. This keeps cold winds from blowing in and helps the house stay warm.

Grass Roof

The grass on a turf house grows like it does on the ground. It has to be cut regularly. Some people use goats!

Above the Arctic Circle, there is no turf. Inuit people of Alaska, northern Canada, Greenland, and Chukotka in the Russian Far East build igloos out of what is available—snow and ice.

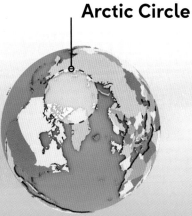

These traditional snow houses are not permanent homes. They are used for emergency shelters and on hunting trips.

Igloos keep out the freezing wind. With an oil lamp inside, they can keep a person or small family safe through the night. Inuit people build igloos as a way to honor the past and pass on their culture.

Cool Place to Stay
Ice hotels are modeled after igloos. Everything inside is made of ice and snow. These hotels melt in the summer, so they must be rebuilt when winter arrives.

Different Ways to Build

Near beaches and waterways, people build houses on stilts or piles. These wooden poles lift homes above the water. They protect homes from flooding when the water level rises.

Making Connections
Kampong Ayer is a 1,000-year-old settlement. Today, 23 miles (37 km) of boardwalks connect 40 small villages.

boardwalk

stilts

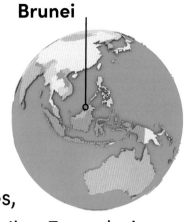

Brunei

People in Kampong Ayer, Brunei, don't just build their homes on stilts. They built their entire settlement—houses, stores, and schools—on stilts. Even their boardwalks stand on stilts that rise out of the water! People walk from building to building on the boardwalks. If they need to travel far, they take boats called water taxis.

High in the Andes Mountains of Peru, the Uros people live on floating islands.

Thousands of years ago, when the Inca invaded their land, the Uros people fled to Lake Titicaca. They did not want to fight. Instead, they built rafts out of reeds growing in the lake. The Uros people escaped onto the rafts and have lived there ever since.

Today, the Uros people fish the lake. They build everything they need from the reeds—houses, furniture, and boats. Every 20 days, villagers add more reeds to refresh the floating islands.

Lake Titicaca, Peru

Houseboats are another kind of floating house. They are popular all over the world, including the southern Indian state of Kerala.

Kerala, India

The traditional Indian houseboats used here are called kettuvallums. They first appeared around 3000 BCE. But they weren't used as homes back then. They were used to transport spices, rice, and people up and down the waterways.

When trains and motor vehicles were invented, all of that stopped. The new types of transportation were much quicker. So, people converted the kettuvallums into homes.

Tied Together
People don't use nails when they build kettuvallam houseboats. Instead, they tie the boats' parts together with coconut fiber ropes.

Earth-Friendly Homes

Many people wish to protect the environment. One way to do that is to build homes out of recycled materials like shipping containers.

Shipping containers are made of thick sheets of steel. They only come in a few sizes—all very large—but they can be arranged like blocks to make homes in different shapes. They can also be used to create apartment buildings.

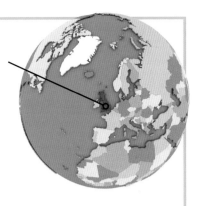

London, England

This apartment building in London, England, is made out of recycled shipping containers. It is called Container City I. Originally, it was three stories high and had 12 apartments where people could live or work. It was so popular that builders added a fourth story with three more spaces. Eighty percent of the structure was made out of recycled materials.

Another eco-friendly option is to use renewable resources like straw. People have been using straw to build houses for centuries. Some homes are made entirely of straw.

Hawaii, USA

Others, like these homes on the island of Hawaii, USA, just have a straw roof.

Energy Saver
The process of making a straw roof is called "thatching." A thatched roof helps control the temperature in a home. That minimizes energy use and lowers monthly bills.

Modern architects recognize the benefits of using straw as a building material. Straw is a lightweight product that grows all over the world. It is made from the dried stalks of harvested grain. When bundled into bales, straw is strong and warm. It doesn't let water in.

Using straw is an eco-friendly way to insulate homes. The houses are often covered with wood or a mud-like mixture to make them stronger.

Builders often borrow design ideas from ancient people. Modern Pueblo people live in the southwestern region of the United States. Long ago, their ancestors lived there, too. They built their homes in the sides of cliffs.

Mesa Verde National Park, Colorado, USA

Nearly all these cliff houses faced south so the winter Sun could heat the surrounding rock. This kept the houses warm at night. During summer, overhanging cliffs blocked the hot Sun and kept the houses cool.

Today, we call this idea passive solar design. Roofs overhang windows and doors. Windows take advantage of sunlight and cooling breezes. Houses are covered in materials that reflect or absorb heat. These features make homes more energy efficient.

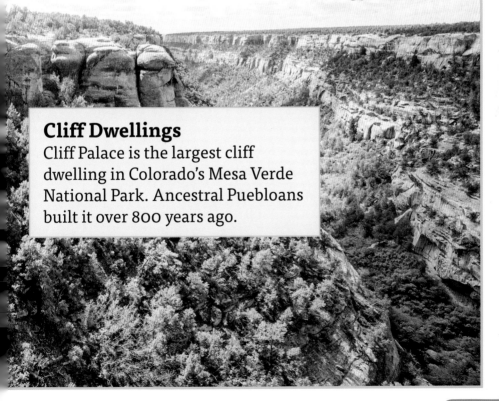

Cliff Dwellings
Cliff Palace is the largest cliff dwelling in Colorado's Mesa Verde National Park. Ancestral Puebloans built it over 800 years ago.

Home Sweet Home

Homes can also tell stories. One of the most famous examples of a storytelling home belongs to the Ndebele people of South Africa.

In the late 19th century, the Ndebele people lost a war. They didn't want to lose their culture, too. So, they began a new tradition. They started painting the walls and gates of their homes. They painted geometric shapes in bold colors outlined with thick black lines. Each shape had a special meaning to the family living there.

Today, the Ndebele people live primarily in the Limpopo and Mpumalanga provinces in South Africa. Families passed down the tradition, and they still decorate their homes in this way.

Limpopo and
Mpumalanga,
South Africa

Houses don't have to be painted in a special way to tell a story. Everything about a home does that—its location, style, size, and shape. The materials used to make a home tell a story, too. They reveal what the environment around the home is like. They are a showcase for the many creative ways people find to design and build a home.

A home tells the story of family. It tells stories about the past and the present. A home can even tell stories about the future and how people are trying to make the world a better place.

Future Homes

Earthship homes are made from natural and recycled materials. They get energy from the Sun and the Earth. They have areas where homeowners can grow their own food. They are self-sustaining homes designed to last well into the future.

Glossary

Absorb
To soak up

Architect
A person who designs buildings

Boardwalk
A walkway made of planks, usually along a beach

Climate
The average weather conditions of a place over a period of time

Culture
The customs and way of life of a group of people

Foundation
The base of a building

Houseboat
A large, usually flat-bottomed boat that is used as a home

Nomadic
Moving from place to place

Passive
Not active, but acted upon

Piles
Long posts made of wood, steel, or concrete used to support buildings

Porcelain
A fine glazed pottery, often from China, used to make dishes and vases

Reflect
To bounce back

Turf
The top layer of soil, held together in a thick mat by grass and other plant roots

Yurt
A light, round tent made of skins or felt that can be easily moved

Index

Quiz

Answer the questions to see what you have learned. Check your answers in the key below.

1. What kind of tent-like home can be easily taken apart and put back together?

2. What is a tongkonan?

3. What are three advantages to living in a cave?

4. How are turf houses made?

5. Where do people build homes on stilts?

6. How are the Uros people able to live on Lake Titicaca?

7. What materials do people use to build earth-friendly homes?

8. Why is passive solar design important?

1. A yurt 2. A traditional wooden home with a boat-shaped roof built by the Toraja people 3. Caves blend into the surroundings, control the temperature, and give people a place to escape from danger 4. With grassy dirt bricks 5. Near water 6. They built floating islands out of reeds 7. Recycled materials and renewable resources 8. It helps people save energy